London Borough of Tower Hamlets

91000008056487

KT-460-096

Living with

A.D.H.D

DR CAI YIMING WITHDRAWN

Marshall Cavendish
Editions

© 2015 Marshall Cavendish International (Asia) Private Limited

Illustrations by Julie Davey
Series designer: Bernard Go

First published 2003 by Times Editions

This 2015 edition published by
Marshall Cavendish Editions
An imprint of Marshall Cavendish International
1 New Industrial Road, Singapore 536196

All rights reserved

No part of this publication may be reproduced, stored in a retrieval system or transmitted, in any form
or by any means, electronic, mechanical, photocopying, recording or otherwise, without the prior
permission of the copyright owner. Requests for permission should be addressed to the Publisher,
Marshall Cavendish International (Asia) Private Limited, 1 New Industrial Road, Singapore 536196.
Tel: (65) 6213 9300, fax: (65) 6285 4871. E-mail: genrefsales@sg.marshallcavendish.com.
Website: www.marshallcavendish.com/genref

The publisher makes no representation or warranties with respect to the contents of this book, and
specifically disclaims any implied warranties or merchantability or fitness for any particular purpose,
and shall in no event be liable for any loss of profit or any other commercial damage, including but not
limited to special, incidental, consequential, or other damages.

Other Marshall Cavendish Offices
Marshall Cavendish Corporation. 99 White Plains Road, Tarrytown NY 10591-9001, USA • Marshall
Cavendish International (Thailand) Co Ltd. 253 Asoke, 12th Flr, Sukhumvit 21 Road, Klongtoey Nua,
Wattana, Bangkok 10110, Thailand • Marshall Cavendish (Malaysia) Sdn Bhd, Times Subang, Lot 46,
Subang Hi-Tech Industrial Park, Batu Tiga, 40000 Shah Alam, Selangor Darul Ehsan, Malaysia

Marshall Cavendish is a trademark of Times Publishing Limited.

National Library Board, Singapore Cataloguing-in-Publication Data
Cai, Yiming, Dr., author.
Living with A.D.H.D / Dr Cai Yiming. – Second edition – Singapore: Marshall Cavendish Editions,
[2015]
pages cm – (Living with)
"First published 2003 by Times Editions."
ISBN: 978-981-4634-16-8 (paperback)

Attention-deficit-disordered children. 2. Attention-deficit hyperactivity disorder. I. Title.
II. Series: Living with.

RJ506.H9
618.928589 — dc23   OCN913077217

Printed in Singapore by Markono Print Media Pte Ltd

Dedicated to
all the children of the Child Guidance Clinic
and their parents

CONTENTS

PREFACE

This book is about children with a particular disorder called Attention Deficit Hyperactivity Disorder (ADHD). Children with ADHD are often in trouble at school. They give parents and teachers a tough time, as they do not complete their homework due to difficulty in focusing on a piece of work. They find it difficult to make friends or get along with peers because they are impulsive and get into fights easily. They are a constant source of stress to teachers and parents.

Parents nowadays are better educated and more aware of mental health issues. They want to do their best and look for early interventions for their children who might have problems impeding their psychological health and academic performance. With the development of a comprehensive community mental health programme in schools called REACH (Response, Early Intervention and Assessment in Community mental Health) by the Ministry of Health, Ministry of Education, Ministry of Social and Family development and the National Council of Social Services working collaboratively, the pick-up rate for ADHD has almost doubled. In 2001 and 2002, the Child Guidance Clinics located at the Health Promotion Board Building and the Institute of Mental Health saw 397 and 457 new cases of children with ADHD respectively (about 15 percent of new cases). In 2012 and 2013, these figures rose sharply to 750 and 654 new cases respectively. ADHD now constitutes 27 to 30 percent of the total number of new consultation cases seen at the clinics.

From a statistical point of view, however, the number of children that turn up for treatment at the clinics is just the tip of the iceberg. In 2013, there were 244,045 primary school students. Among these children, statistics show that 4 to 5 percent will have ADHD. If we take an average of 4.5 percent of 244,045 students, as many as 10,980 primary school students may have ADHD. In practical terms, this means that one to two students in an average primary school class of 35 students may have ADHD. From this, we may conclude that many children with ADHD are not recognised and brought to the attention of mental health professionals.

Dr Cai Yiming
July 2015

INTRODUCTION

To many parents, coping with one child with Attention Deficit Hyperactivity Disorder (ADHD) is difficult enough. Coping with two children with ADHD means significant increases in their problems. This is because the likelihood of children in a family having ADHD is fairly high; the effect of having two children with ADHD is often not equal to twice as many problems, but 11 times as many problems.

ADHD children also pose a challenge for the mental health professionals who treat them. This is because diagnosing the disorder is complex as there are various other mental conditions, such as depression, that could account for the restlessness and concentration difficulties in the child. The child may then be misdiagnosed as having ADHD. Also, these other conditions can exist alongside ADHD in a child. It is therefore crucial that any analysis or evaluation of an inattentive and hyperactive child is done carefully by professionals so that the diagnosis is accurate and the child is treated appropriately.

This book highlights the complexity of diagnosis and discusses various aspects of ADHD — its presentation, causes and treatment, the misconceptions surrounding it and the latest research findings. Considerable emphasis is put on how parents and teachers can help children with ADHD more promptly and effectively, thereby reducing suffering and distress of all parties.

I hope the book will serve as a useful reference guide for parents, teachers and healthcare workers. I hope it also spurs the reader into looking for more information either on the Internet or from books. This is especially relevant as developments in research and clinical practice are rapidly expanding, with new findings and exciting ideas appearing that might influence the outcome of treatment for ADHD.

WHAT IS ATTENTION DEFICIT HYPERACTIVITY DISORDER (ADHD)?

PART 1

Attention Deficit Hyperactivity Disorder (ADHD) is a neuro-developmental disorder of self-control. As the name suggests, the symptoms of ADHD are characterised by serious and persistent difficulties in three areas, namely:

- inattention,
- impulsivity,
- hyperactivity.

ADHD is a neuro-developmental disorder in the sense that it arises early in child development, before the age of 12. ADHD is related to abnormalities in brain functioning and development. It is also associated with other factors that can affect brain functioning or development such as genetic factors, injuries, toxins and infections. Boys tend to be affected more than girls by a ratio of three or four to one.

1.1   MY CHILD IS 6 YEARS OLD. HE IS EXTREMELY ACTIVE AND RUNS ABOUT AT HOME. DOES IT MEAN HE HAS ADHD?

It is normal for children to be active, inattentive and impulsive. Developmentally, this is understandable and should not be a cause for concern for parents. In fact, about one-third of children are described by their parents as overactive and between 5 percent and 20 percent of schoolchildren are described as such by their teachers. Among these schoolchildren, however, it is likely that 3 percent to 5 percent have ADHD.

If your child is getting on well socially with other children and teachers, picking up in learning, is not distressed about school and does not cause disruptive behaviour in school or other social settings, then it is unlikely that your child has ADHD.

The key here is whether your child has serious and pervasive impairment in social, learning and behavioural functions that are maladaptive and inconsistent for a child of his age.

1.2   WHAT SYMPTOMS DO CHILDREN WITH ADHD PRESENT?

Children with ADHD exhibit a variety of symptoms. ADHD begins in childhood. According to diagnostic criteria on the next page, the symptoms must have started before the age of 12 and be evident for at least six months.

With inattention, the child:
- often fails to give close attention to details,
- often has difficulty sustaining attention in tasks or play activities,
- is often easily distracted by extraneous stimuli,
- is often forgetful in daily activities,
- often does not seem to listen when spoken to directly,
- makes careless mistakes in schoolwork or other activities,
- often does not follow instructions and fails to finish schoolwork, chores or duties (not due to defiant behaviour or failure to understand instructions),
- often has difficulty organising tasks and activities,
- often avoids, dislikes or is reluctant to engage in tasks that require sustained mental effort (schoolwork or homework),
- often loses things necessary for tasks or activities (toys, school assignments, pencils, books or tools).

With hyperactivity and impulsivity, the child:
- often fidgets or squirms in the seat,
- often leaves his seat in the classroom or in other situations where remaining seated is expected,
- often runs about or climbs excessively in situations where it is inappropriate,
- often has difficulty playing or engaging in leisure activities quietly,
- is often "on the go" or often acts as if he is "driven by a motor",
- often talks excessively,
- often blurts out answers before questions have been completed,
- often has difficulty waiting for his turn,
- often interrupts or intrudes on others.

The diagnostic criteria was established in the Diagnostic and Statistical Manual, 5th edition (DSM-5), American Psychiatric Association (2013). The DSM is one of two major classifications psychiatrists use today. It is used officially in the US and adopted in many countries.

The International Classification of Diseases, 10th edition (ICD-10) by WHO (World Health Organisation) is the other major classification.

1.3   HOW ARE CHILDREN WITH ADHD DIFFERENT FROM NORMAL CHILDREN?

As can be seen from the list in 1.2, children with ADHD are clearly distinguished from normal children in many respects. Their problems are pervasive and occur across different social situations, affecting their ability to function successfully for age-appropriate demands. Their problems are also persistent over time and are not caused by environmental or social factors.

1.4   ARE CHILDREN WITH ADHD MORE PRONE TO INJURIES?

Children with ADHD are impulsive. They often begin tasks before receiving adequate instruction, and are thus likely to make careless errors and take unnecessary risks. People who are unaware of the disorder are likely to label these children as irresponsible and immature. Research studies show that children with ADHD tend to have more accidents than normal children of the same age.

1.5   ARE THERE DIFFERENT TYPES OF ADHD?

In the DSM-4 (published in 1994), there are five sub-types of ADHD:

- Predominantly Hyperactivity-Impulsive,
- Predominantly Inattentive,
- Mixed/Combined,
- In Partial Remission,
- Not Otherwise Specified.

Most children have symptoms of the Mixed/Combined type. However, there are some children with either the Predominantly Hyperactivity-Impulsive type or the Predominantly Inattentive type. It is noteworthy that children with the Predominantly Inattentive type of ADHD tend to daydream and have difficultly focusing on their tasks. They are, however, not hyperactive.

A small number of children falls into the other two categories. Individuals, especially adolescents and adults, who currently have symptoms that no longer meet the full criteria, fall into the In Partial Remission type. Individuals are considered Not Otherwise Specified if they do not meet the criteria in full in either of the symptom clusters of the Predominantly Inattentive category or the Predominantly Hyperactivity-Impulsive category.

However, it must be noted that in the DSM-5, the five sub-types are no longer differentiated. Instead, the DSM-5 emphasises the current clinical presentation of ADHD, which may be hyperactive-impulsive, inattentive or combined. This has arisen from research showing that ADHD symptoms may change over time (e.g. from predominantly combined symptoms to predominantly inattentive symptoms).

1.6   WHAT WOULD HAPPEN TO CHILDREN WHO ARE UNRECOGNISED AND UNTREATED FOR ADHD?

Children with ADHD will suffer needlessly if they are untreated. Furthermore, the consequences for them are significant. They are likely to lose interest in studies and have low self-esteem. They may also find it difficult to make friends.

They Lose Interest In Studies

Children with ADHD do not lack intelligence. But they tend to fall behind in their studies because they are unable to focus on the task at hand. When they fail to listen to instructions, they resort to telling lies, which often leads to punishment by parents or teachers. This has the undesired consequence of creating a dislike of school and a loss of interest in their studies.

They Have Poor Self-Esteem

Teachers and parents who do not know of this disorder are likely to consider children with unruly behaviour as purposely defiant and uncooperative. Instead of perceiving the child as unthinkingly breaching rules in school or at home, they may scold him and label him as naughty, undisciplined or lazy. The child is often receiving unfair criticism and is being unnecessarily punished by teachers and parents. It is thus easy to see why many children with ADHD have low self-esteem.

They Do Not Have Many Friends

ADHD is often a cause of strained relationships. The child is often seen by his classmates and peers as undisciplined and rude. He is also more likely to get into fights with them. The result is rejection and dislike by his peers.

CASE STUDY

WHY CAN'T HE JUST STOP?

Julian Tan is seven years old. He was brought to the Child Guidance Clinic by his desperate parents to seek help for his hyperactive behaviour. "Why can't he just stop?" asked his mother in exasperation. In tow also was Jonathan, Julian's seven-month-old brother.

According to his parents, Julian has always been an active boy, even in infancy. Although constantly involved in some activity, he is never able to pursue the activity to completion. He is disruptive in the classroom and often fails to hand in his homework. He also gets into fights with the other boys in his class frequently.

At the clinic, Julian was restless and constantly paced about the room. In his mother's arms, Jonathan was squirming, kicking his legs and stretching his arms. His parents reported that Jonathan is more active than Julian was at that age and requires very little sleep.

This is a classic case of ADHD with early onset and a family history. With drug treatment and behaviour management therapy, Julian soon settled down in the classroom and at home.

CHANGING CONCEPTS OF ADHD
AND EARLY TREATMENT

PART 2

In 1902, British paediatrician George Still described a group of twenty children who had problems similar to what we now diagnose as Attention Deficit Hyperactivity Disorder (ADHD) and Conduct Disorder. It was the first description that identified a disorder of impulse control and inattention. He recorded that these children had a "defect of moral control". In other words, they failed to control their behaviour despite knowing that what they did was wrong. He also noted that these children:

- required immediate gratification without regard to others,
- were restless and impulsive,
- had attention problems,
- had strong emotions (usually anger and hostility which would lead to fights or destruction of things),
- were dishonest and cruel,
- often broke the law.

2.1   HOW DID THE MEDICAL MODEL COME ABOUT?

The question in Still's mind was whether these problems of inattention and impulse control were inherent in the children. If they were, it meant that the children had little control of their impulses. In this sense, the children were not "bad" to start with and should not be blamed or punished for their misbehaviour. Instead, they should be regarded as having a medical disorder. With this reasoning, Still shifted the inattention and impulsivity from the moral sphere (laziness, bad behaviour, lack of discipline) to a medical model to account for the children's misbehaviour.

However, many people did not agree with the model. They saw such misbehaviour in children as laziness and disobedience that should be dealt with by discipline and not treated as a medical disorder with drugs. Instead of being dealt with firmly, these children were seen as being protected by the medical profession and excused on medical grounds. This controversy is still not resolved and continues to be actively debated.

2.2   WHAT OTHER KEY DEVELOPMENTS HELPED DOCTORS UNDERSTAND ADHD?

Co-morbid Conditions

Children with ADHD often display associated features of disturbances in learning, mood and conduct that are not the core symptoms of ADHD. They may frequently have other mental conditions, such as conduct disorder, anxiety, tics or disruptive disorders, existing at the same time. These features have raised the concept of co-morbid conditions or conditions that exist together. Active research into these areas is currently being pursued and more findings are expected to surface in the near future.

Brain Damage

In the 1920s, two major developments gave rise to the view that attention problems and restlessness could have had an organic origin.

The first was the influenza pandemic that followed World War I and the epidemic of encephalitis lethargica, a viral infection of the brain, that occurred in Europe between 1918 and 1926. Doctors found that children who survived these infections frequently developed a severe behavioural disorder similar to that described by Still in 1902.

The other influential development occurred in the 1930s to 1940s. During this period, doctors described a link between severe brain damage and restlessness in retarded children and adults. Other doctors also began to emphasise the organic cause by describing retarded children as hyperactive, easily distracted and impulsive. These children faced difficulties processing information and interpreting events in their environment. The children were considered to be brain-damaged even though no visible damage in their brains was observed. These children were diagnosed as having the "Minimal Brain Damage Syndrome".

Minimal Brain Dysfunction

In 1962, the medical community endorsed the term "Minimal Brain Dysfunction" at an international conference held in the UK. Instead of the idea of brain damage, the term introduced the concept of some disorder in the brains of these children. When faced with adversity, the disorder led to an abnormal function of the brain. This new term was an improvement over the "Minimal Brain Damage Syndrome" and had immense popularity. However, its usage did not last and the term was eventually discarded.

Hyperkinetic Disorder Of Childhood

The next important landmark in classifying this disorder occurred in the 1960s with the introduction of the term "Hyperkinetic Disorder of Childhood". This term was adopted by the International Classification of Diseases (ICD) and by the Diagnostic and Statistical Manual (DSM). The DSM is used in the US, whereas the ICD is used predominantly in non-American western countries. While the term "Hyperkinetic Disorder" is still retained in the ICD, the DSM moved on to use another term.

2.3 HOW AND WHEN DID THE CONCEPT OF ADHD TAKE ROOT?

In 1980, the term "Hyperkinetic Disorder of Childhood" was renamed to Attention Deficit Disorder with Hyperactivity (ADDH) or without Hyperactivity (ADD). This new term was introduced in the DSM-3.

The aim was to distinguish attention problems from the hyperactivity problems. In ADDH, all three cardinal symptoms of inattention, impulsivity and hyperactivity were present, whereas ADD required only the presence of inattention and impulsivity.

2.4 WHEN WAS THE TERM ADHD INTRODUCED OFFICIALLY?

The distinction between ADDH and ADD was short-lived and the term was again revised to Attention Deficit Hyperactivity Disorder (ADHD). This revision was made in DSM-3 R (1987) and its use is retained in DSM-4 (1994).

With this new term, the co-existence of inattention and hyperactivity in the disorder were recognised. This new system of classification has had a profound influence on clinical practice. It led to an increase in the recognition of the disorder in the community, the development of various forms of treatment and a tremendous interest in research work.

2.5 WHAT WERE THE EARLY DRUG TREATMENTS?

Early drug treatments began with an interesting observation of the effects of a stimulant drug that was given to a group of children with behavioural problems.

In 1937, doctors gave some children at the Emma Pendleton Bradley Residential Treatment Center in Rhode Island, US, a stimulant called Benzedrine (d- and l-amphetamine). They discovered that the drug not only reduced restlessness, it also improved concentration and motivation in the children.

Thirty years later, in a research study in 1967, doctors used another stimulant, dextro-amphetamine, to treat a group of adolescents with behavioural problems. This study confirmed the effectiveness of stimulant drug treatment.

Since then, many clinical trials have been conducted on a large group of children. All these trials show without doubt that stimulant drug treatment for ADHD is safe and effective in the short and intermediate term.

2.6   IN WHAT DIRECTIONS IS SCIENTIFIC RESEARCH MOVING TO EXPAND OUR KNOWLEDGE OF ADHD?

Since 1996, our knowledge of ADHD has been rapidly expanding with many research studies that were carried out along four directions:

- Studies that focus on a wider range of patients — these include those below six years old; adolescents and young adults; and those with ADHD plus at least one other disorder (co-morbid populations).
- Studies that look for new drug treatments — types of stimulants and other new medications.
- Studies that look into different types and combinations of treatment rather than stimulant drug treatment alone.
- Extending the ADHD age-of-onset criterion to age 12

With regard to studies that look into various combinations of treatment, one particular study deserves a special mention. This is the Multimodal Treatment of Children with ADHD Study or MTA Study. The MTA Study is the most expensive and largest clinical trial ever conducted by the National Institute of Mental Health in the US. More details of the important findings from this study can be found in Part 14 of this book.

2.7   AGE OF ONSET OF ADHD

ADHD begins in childhood. The age at symptom onset used to be before 7 years old. However, the DSM-5, published in 2013, has pushed the age to before 12 years old.

This amendment largely arose from studies involving the diagnosis of ADHD in adult patients where there was difficulty obtaining retrospective information about the presence of ADHD symptoms prior to age 7. There were studies reporting that adults who were able to report symptom onset by age 12 also had symptoms by age 7, even if they could not report them.

It is also to be noted that in preschool, the main manifestation is hyperactivity and to many parents this may be considered as "normal" behavior for a toddler below 4 years old. ADHD is most often identified during the primary school years (age 6 to 12) when inattention becomes more prominent and impairing with increasing academic and social demands.

2.8   BRAIN MATURITY IN CHILDREN WITH ADHD

In children with ADHD, the brain matures in a normal pattern but is delayed by three years in some regions, on average, compared to children without the disorder. This was revealed by an imaging study by researchers at the US National Institutes of Health's (NIH) National Institute of Mental Health (NIMH).

The delay due to ADHD was most prominent in regions at the front of the brain's outer mantle (cortex), which is important for the ability to control thinking, attention and planning.

"Finding a normal pattern of cortex maturation, albeit delayed, in children with ADHD should be reassuring to families and could help to explain why many youth eventually seem to grow out of the disorder," explained Philip Shaw, M.D., NIMH Child Psychiatry Branch, who led the research team. The magnetic resonance imaging (MRI) study was reported in November 2007 in the online edition of the Proceedings of the National Academy of Sciences.

However, brain imaging is still not ready for use as a diagnostic tool in ADHD. The delay in cortex development could be detected only when a very large number of children with the disorder were included. It is not yet possible to detect such delay from the brain scans of just one individual. The diagnosis of ADHD remains clinical, based on considering the history of the child from his family and teachers.

COMMON MISCONCEPTIONS ABOUT ADHD

PART 3

Whenever there is ignorance or a lack of understanding or knowledge about a condition, people start to wonder and think of all sorts of possibilities. While some of the thoughts are absurd and far-fetched, they can become deeply entrenched in the mind as beliefs. The beliefs may be passed down from generation to generation. These beliefs form the basis of the myths and misconceptions about Attention Deficit Hyperactivity Disorder (ADHD).

The consequences of adhering to such beliefs can be disastrous for a child with ADHD and harmful to the parent-child relationship This is because:

- the child would not receive proper diagnosis and treatment,
- labelling the child incorrectly would lead to wrong methods of handling by parents and teachers (e.g. a child with ADHD whose inattentive behaviour is viewed as laziness might be reprimanded with a cane),
- wrong labelling has the unintended effect of a self-fulfilling prophecy. If a child is labelled as lazy, there is really nothing much the child can do but to behave according to the way he is seen.

Let us look at some common misconceptions about children with ADHD.

3.1   ADHD IS A SIGN OF SOME SORT OF INHERENT BADNESS IN THE CHILD

Although research findings show that ADHD tends to run in families, it is not a sort of badness that is being passed down in the child. Children with ADHD are not characterised by the propensity to be bad or naughty. They might appear to be mischievous and show a lack of control in impulsive acts, but the intention to do harm is not present.

3.2   ADHD IS CAUSED BY SOMETHING THE CHILD HAS EATEN

There is no scientific evidence to show that food can give rise to ADHD. It is worth remembering that ADHD arises early in life when the main diet of the child is mainly milk and water, followed by oats and cereals. These foods are not known to cause ADHD. However, some foods might cause allergies which may lead to changes in behaviour. In these instances, the changed behaviour is episodic and in direct relation to the time of ingestion of the food. Stopping the offending food would bring about immediate relief. Food as a cause of ADHD is extremely rare.

3.3   ADHD IS A TEMPORARY STATE THAT WILL BE OUTGROWN

It is not correct to think that ADHD is a temporary state. Some milder cases of ADHD may remit or abate in late childhood or early teens. But the more severe cases can continue into late adolescence and even adulthood with serious social, academic and occupational impairment. Sufferers of ADHD have gone on to be involved in substance abuse and criminal activities. Delay in bringing the child for treatment may cause severe impairment in academic and social functions that are beyond reversal.

3.4   ADHD IS A TRYING BUT NORMAL PHASE OF CHILDHOOD

ADHD is not a normal phase of childhood. The disorder has significant impact on the child's development, learning, and self-esteem because it persists across different social settings. All these significant impairments do not support the idea that it is a trying but normal phase of childhood. Its adverse consequences have been shown to persist in the long term and, in some cases, into adulthood.

3.5   ADHD IS A RESPONSE TO BORING LESSONS IN CLASSROOMS

Children may not pay attention to lessons that are boring but this inattention is understandable and applies to most children. This type of inattention should not be taken as a symptom of ADHD. If this is so, then all of us would have had ADHD since we would have been inattentive in class at one point or another.

On the contrary, a child with ADHD would still be inattentive even if the lessons are interesting and hold the attention of the majority of the children in the class. It is this type of difference in behaviour that distinguishes the child from normalcy and points to the likelihood that the child might have ADHD.

3.6   THE ADHD CHILD IS LAZY AND DOES NOT TRY HIS BEST

Contrary to this belief, ADHD children can be hardworking but they lack focus and are unable to complete tasks. In fact, these children work on too many projects at one time and fail to complete any of them satisfactorily.

Some children with ADHD will do well in tasks that interest them and do not tax their attention skills to the fullest. For example, some ADHD children seem to do well in sporting and outdoor activities like trekking or mountain climbing.

ADHD children are seen as intelligent. Despite this, they are often mistakenly labelled as lazy because they fail to meet up to the expectations of their parents or teachers. The ADHD child is not lazy or not trying his best. He simply cannot perform his best because of his crippling ADHD symptoms.

3.7 ADHD IS CAUSED BY PARENTAL FAILURE TO DISCIPLINE OR CONTROL THE CHILD

Many parents wonder if they have failed to discipline or control the child. They might blame themselves for not being able to rein in their child from "misbehaving". It is not defective parenting skills or the lack of discipline that contribute to the development of ADHD in children.

3.8 THE ADHD CHILD IS A PRODUCT OF A MODERN SOCIETY

There are two arguments to support the idea that children with ADHD are not a product of today's society. First, the child with ADHD shows signs of having a short attention span early, in the first seven years of life before he is even exposed or needs to adapt to the many aspects of modern society. Second, it is a fact that there were children with ADHD long before the arrival of modern life.

3.9 ADHD IS A RESULT OF BEING POSSESSED BY EVIL SPIRITS OR THE "MONKEY GOD"

Parents who are influenced by cultural beliefs might think that their child is being possessed by an evil spirit or a "monkey god" when they see the child jumping about and displaying restlessness. The parents might then bring the child to a temple medium for "treatment".

3.10 ADHD IS CAUSED BY POOR PARENTING STYLES

There are basically three main parenting styles:
- Authoritarian (giving orders).
- Permissive (giving in).
- Authoritative (giving directions).

Most parents tend to start with an authoritarian style when the child is young. When the child grows older, enlightened parents adjust their expectations and adopt the authoritative style. What is unhelpful is to practise inconsistent styles of parenting as this only confuses the child. Parents should try to coordinate their parenting styles so that children are clear about what is expected of them.

Parenting styles, if not practised appropriately and in accordance with the child's level of development and understanding, might confuse the child. But parenting styles by themselves do not make the child impulsive, inattentive and hyperactive, which are the main characteristics of children with ADHD.

Types of parenting styles

- Authoritarian — This style of parenting is very strict. Children are kept in line with rewards and punishment. The problem with this style is that children may learn to expect rewards for being good. Overly harsh punishments may create excessive fear and resentment. However, this is still a highly effective form of parenting for young children whose understanding is literal and simplistic.
- Permissive — Parents who adopt this style set no limits and children grow up with no guidelines. These children are often seen as "spoilt". The problem with this style is that children are unaware of their social responsibilities and will have difficulty learning how to behave in society. This is probably the worst form of parenting.
- Authoritative — This parenting style is based on understanding and respecting children. Parents who adopt this style provide guidance that fit the child's age and development. They encourage discussions of problems, give rational explanations for decisions governing rules at home and respect participation in decision-making. Yet, they retain ultimate responsibility. Such parents also value good behaviour and proper conduct.

THE CAUSES OF ADHD

PART 4

Attention Deficit Hyperactivity Disorder (ADHD) is a neuro-developmental disorder. In ADHD, certain chemicals in the brain, especially dopamine, are not working properly. The exact cause of ADHD is not known but doctors have attributed the causes to five main factors, namely:

- family and genetic factors,
- factors before and during birth,
- chemical toxins,
- psychosocial stressors,
- abnormalities in brain structure and function.

4.1   HOW ARE FAMILY AND GENETIC FACTORS IMPLICATED IN ADHD?

ADHD tends to run in families and genetic influences are likely to play a role in its causation. Research studies show that in the families of children with ADHD, 25 percent of first degree relatives (where there is a direct and close link in genes such as between parents and their children) also had a history of ADHD compared with only 5 percent of those in unaffected families. Furthermore, a significant proportion of parents whose children were diagnosed with ADHD believed they (the parents) could have had ADHD themselves when they were younger but were unaware of it as they were undiagnosed.

The most conclusive evidence that genetics can contribute to ADHD comes from studies of twins. In these studies, the ADHD risk of a child whose identical twin has the disorder is between 11 and 18 times greater than that of a non-twin sibling of a child with ADHD. Between 55 percent and 92 percent of identical twins of affected children will eventually develop ADHD. These studies demonstrate the importance of a genetic influence. The closer the blood ties, the higher the risk.

4.2   WHAT ABOUT FACTORS JUST BEFORE AND DURING THE BIRTH OF THE CHILD?

Mothers of ADHD children are more likely to have had a lengthy labour and delivery or complications of pregnancy, such as toxaemia. Toxaemia is a serious medical condition in which the mother develops high blood pressure before and around the time of birth of her child. The high blood pressure reduces the flow of blood to the foetus, which in turn may damage its brain. The condition might call for an early Caesarean surgical intervention to deliver the child so as to minimise any damage to it in the womb.

There is also some speculation that a difficult childbirth might bring about some damage to the brain of the child. For example, approximately 20 percent of children who sustain severe traumatic brain injury before or during birth have a subsequent onset of substantial symptoms of impulsivity and inattention.

4.3   WHAT ABOUT CHEMICAL TOXINS?

Various toxic chemical agents — whether they come from the environment or are present in food additives or in some therapeutically administered medications — have been implicated in ADHD.

One example of an environmental toxin is lead. Research studies show that high levels of exposure to lead and in cumulative doses are related to problems of aggression and attention difficulties.

In administered medications, the use of phenobarbitone as an anti-epilepsy drug might bring about hyperactive behaviour in the child. With regard to the causative role of toxins found in dietary substances like food additives and sugar, these have not been proven and very few cases can be accounted for. On the whole, the research findings on the role of toxins in food substances are not convincing.

4.4   CAN PSYCHOSOCIAL STRESSORS IN THE FAMILY CAUSE ADHD?

Family problems, such as parents under stress from work or poor spousal relationships, do not cause ADHD in children per se. But it is likely that children with ADHD may have their symptoms worsened if they live in a family where there is marital discord or where the parents have mental disorders. This is because these parents are less able to take care of and effectively control their children who already have ADHD.

Studies show that there is a correlation in the severity of the symptoms in ADHD children to the levels of stress and social adversity in their families. The risk of having an increased range of co-morbid conditions like depression, anxiety and general psychosocial dysfunction in these children are also reported.

4.5   TO WHAT EXTENT ARE ABNORMALITIES IN BRAIN STRUCTURES OR FUNCTIONS A CAUSE OF ADHD?

Over the last twenty years, specialised techniques such as magnetic resonance imaging (MRI) and positron-emission tomography (PET) have made it possible to study the brain to find out if there are any structural or functional abnormalities in children with ADHD:

- Tests using these techniques show that in children with ADHD:
- There are fairly consistent findings of altered structures and functions in three parts of the brain—the prefrontal cortex, basal ganglia and cerebellum.
- There is a loss of normal brain symmetry. The two hemispheres of the brain are not in the balanced and identical positions as one would see one's face in the mirror.
- The volumes of the specific structures—the prefrontal cortex, basal ganglia and cerebellum—in the brain are small. However, the estimated difference of these structural changes in children with ADHD and in normal children is only about 5 percent to 10 percent smaller. This difference is not significant and limits the usefulness of using these specialised techniques to diagnose ADHD.

4.6 WHAT FUNCTION DOES THE NEUROTRANSMITTER DOPAMINE SERVE? HOW DO WE KNOW THAT THE ABNORMALITIES LIE WITH DOPAMINE?

The brain depends on dopamine to function properly. Three areas of the brain in particular—the prefrontal cortex, basal ganglia and cerebellum—are rich in dopamine receptors. In individuals with ADHD, doctors have found altered structures and functions in these areas. However, when pyscho-stimulant drugs were given, they were found to act on these very areas which led to improvement in behaviour.

Because most of the psycho-stimulant drugs that are used for treating ADHD act on these sites, many investigators have found support for the dopamine site-of-action hypothesis. In view of this understanding, current medical treatment for ADHD involves the use of stimulant drugs which act on these sites in the brain.

ASSOCIATED DISORDERS OF ADHD

PART 5

Attention Deficit Hyperactivity Disorder (ADHD) is frequently co-morbid (exists together) with a variety of other psychiatric disorders such as conduct disorders and tic disorder. Doctors will attempt to rule out all these other disorders as they can also lead to inattention and hyperactivity. For these reasons, it is not advisable for parents to self-diagnose their children for ADHD. This section describes some of the other disorders.

5.1   WHAT ARE CONDUCT DISORDERS?

Conduct disorders are a complicated group of behavioural and emotional problems. Children and adolescents with conduct disorders have great difficulty following rules and behaving in a socially acceptable way. The causes of conduct disorders include brain damage, child abuse, failure in school, and negative family and social experiences.

The symptoms of conduct disorders include:
- an inability to control anger,
- physical and verbal aggression with people,
- lying and stealing,
- destroying property,
- sexual misbehaviour.

The result is that individuals with conduct disorders are often viewed by others as bad or delinquent, rather than mentally ill. The child's "bad" behaviour causes a negative reaction from others, which makes the child behave even more "badly".

Studies show that youngsters who do not receive early, ongoing and comprehensive treatment like behaviour therapy are unable to adapt to the demands of adulthood. They continue to have problems with relationships and holding a job. Many children with a conduct disorder may be diagnosed as also having a co-existing depression or an attention deficit disorder.

CASE STUDY

ADHD WITH CO-MORBID CONDUCT DISORDER

Kelvin is a Secondary One student. He was referred to the Child Guidance Clinic by the police when they arrested him for selling illegal VCDs.

Interviews with his teachers revealed that Kelvin was inattentive, talkative, disruptive, defiant and argumentative. He could not to stay seated during lessons. However, his teachers report that his school performance was fairly good despite some difficulties with reading and writing. On the home front, Kelvin's relationship with his parents was strained. He was rebellious and defiant. He would return home late or stay out the whole night without informing his parents. On the whole, his thinking and behaviour was immature and he had little control over his emotions.

With medication, counselling and family work, Kelvin's behaviour improved. He is more caring and receptive to advice given by his parents. His relationship with his peers at school also improved.

Kelvin has ADHD with conduct disorder as a co-morbid disorder.

5.2   WHAT IS OPPOSITIONAL DEFIANT DISORDER?

This is a type of conduct disorder which is characteristically seen in younger children below the age of 10. It is defined by the presence of markedly defiant, disobedient, provocative behaviour, and the absence of more severe anti-social or aggressive acts that violate the law or the rights of others. Examples of these acts are stealing, cruelty, bullying and destroying property.

Children with this disorder:

- frequently defy adults and deliberately annoy other people,
- tend to be angry, resentful, rude and uncooperative,
- are easily annoyed by other people whom they blame for their own mistakes or difficulties,
- get frustrated very easily and readily lose their temper. Typically, their defiance has a provocative quality so that they initiate confrontations.

Such behaviour is most evident in interactions with adults or peers whom the child knows well. This disorder could be considered as a mild form of conduct disorder. As with conduct disorders, treatment involves psychotherapy and behavior therapy.

5.3 WHAT ARE ANXIETY DISORDERS?

All children experience emotions. Anxiety in children is expected and normal at specific times of development. For example, between the ages of 7 months to the preschool years, healthy youngsters may show intense distress or anxiety at times of separation from persons with whom they are close.

Anxious children may also have short-lived fears of strangers, animals or the dark. They are often overly tense or uptight and their worries may interfere with activities. Some may seek a lot of reassurance.

Some anxious children may also be quiet, compliant and eager to please. Because of this their difficulties may be missed.

When emotions become severe and begin to interfere with the daily activities of childhood, such as attending school and making friends, the evaluation and advice of a child psychiatrist may be necessary.

Children with severe anxiety disorder should be treated early to prevent complications. Early treatment through therapy and counselling can prevent future difficulties such as loss of friendships, failure to reach social and academic potential, and feelings of low self-esteem.

Symptoms of severe separation anxiety include:

- constant thoughts and fears about safety of self and parents,
- refusing to go to school,
- frequent stomach-aches and other physical complaints,
- extreme worries about sleeping away from home,
- overly clingy behaviour at home,
- panic or tantrums at times of separation from parents,
- fear of meeting or talking to new people (children with this difficulty may have few friends outside the family),
- many worries about things before they happen,
- constant worries or concern, for instance, about school or friends.

5.4   WHAT ARE MOOD DISORDERS?

Children who suffer from mood disorders could go into any of three states—a low mood, an elevated mood, or a mixture of both. The child has depression if the mood is low. If the mood is heightened excessively, it becomes mania. Children who have episodes both of mania and depression are categorised as suffering from a manic-depressive illness.

The symptoms of depression include:

• feeling sad and miserable most of the time,
• diminished interest in nearly all activities,
• loss of energy,
• sleep problems (either sleeping too much or too little),
• irritability, restlessness or slowing down in the child's behaviour,
• failure to gain expected weight with loss of appetite,
• feeling guilty and worthless,
• inability to concentrate or think clearly.

Depression is treated with individual and group therapy. These aim to help the child cope with the depression through stress management and problem-solving skills, as well as help the child's parents reduce environmental stressors. If the depression is severe and debilitating and the child is older, a short course of medication can help.

Mania is a serious illness characterised by:

• an elevated mood,
• flight of ideas,
• restlessness and excessive talking,
• increased physical and mental energy and activity.

Children with mania often experience marked feelings of grandiosity and well-being. Their concentration and attention are impaired, which makes it difficult for them to settle down to rest or do any meaningful work. They may spend money excessively by buying things they do not need. They also appear to be over-familiar with strangers.

The treatment of mania requires aggressive and judicious use of drugs to immediately control and abort the symptoms. Mania often continues into adult life. Mania and manic-depressive disorders often necessitate long-term treatment with drugs.

5.5   WHAT IS A TIC DISORDER?

A tic is a problem in which a part of the body moves repeatedly, quickly, suddenly and uncontrollably. Tics can occur in the face, hands or legs. They can be stopped voluntarily for brief periods. Sounds that are made involuntarily are called vocal tics. Most tics are mild and hardly noticeable. However, where they are frequent and severe, the disorder can affect many areas of a child's life.

The most common tic disorder is called transient tic disorder, which may affect up to 10 percent of children during the early school years. People who notice the tics may wonder if the child is nervous or under stress. Transient tics go away by themselves. Some tics, however, do not go away. Tics which last one year or more are called chronic tics. These affect less than 1 percent of children and may be related to a special, more unusual tic disorder called Tourette's Disorder.

Tourette's Disorder

Children with Tourette's Disorder may have both body and vocal tics. They may act impulsively, or they may develop obsessions and compulsions. Sometimes they may blurt out obscene words, insult others, or make obscene gestures or movements. They cannot control these sounds and movements and should not be blamed for them. Punishment by parents, teasing by classmates and scolding by teachers will not help the child to control the tics but will only hurt the child's self-esteem.

5.6   WHAT ARE LEARNING DISORDERS?

Learning problems in young children are difficult to identify. A child may be called a slow learner for a variety of reasons. Parents may mistakenly label the child as lazy, stubborn, defiant, stupid or even mentally ill.

Let us first examine the concept of a slow learner. Slowness implies that a child is essentially normal except in learning. How slow must a child be before he is considered a slow learner? This is an arbitrary level determined by the majority of children. In statistics, a slow learner would be a child, if the learning abilities of a population of children were measured, who falls into the last 2.5 percent.

There are four factors that might independently or interactively produce a slow learner, namely:
- learning disorders,
- parental expectations,
- the underachieving child,
- intellectual disability.

Learning Disorders

Learning disorders are defined as specific learning difficulties in the areas of reading, writing or arithmetic that is significantly below what is expected of a child. These learning disorders occur in spite of a normal intelligence and adequate exposure to learning. They are not due to any physical disabilities such as severe asthma or epilepsy that prevents the child from learning. The most common learning disorder is a specific reading disorder which is frequently known by the name, dyslexia.

Children with learning disorders display many of the features that resemble ADHD. These include difficulty in concentrating and focusing, frustration and loss of temper with impulsive acts. However, the single most outstanding feature that differentiates a child with learning disorders from one with ADHD is that the former often manifests emotional and behavioural difficulties only in a classroom situation. In the home and unless he is required to study, he is relatively well-behaved and appears normal to parents.

Parental Expectations

The expectations that parents have of their children can have unintended effects on the child. For instance, some parents may not consider their child's performance in school as good enough even though the child is performing in accordance with his ability and age. Such parents may push the child to perform above his abilities. All this only leads to anxiety and disappointment in the parents, and unnecessary stress for the child.

The Underachieving Child

The underachieving child is one who may have been denied some of the foundations of learning. An example is the child who missed preschool because his parents felt it was unnecessary. While this may have been acceptable in the past, it is not so today because young children these days must have some basic training before starting formal school. Preschool education aims to provide just that.

Intellectual Disability

An intellectual disability refers to low intellectual functioning and is demonstrated by IQ scores approximately below 70 using a standard intelligence test. Symptoms of ADHD are common among children placed in academic settings that are inappropriate to their intellectual ability. They are better placed in special schools where non-academic vocational skills are emphasised and their symptoms would not be as evident.

5.7 AUTISM SPECTRUM DISORDER (ASD)

Children with ADHD and those with ASD exhibit inattention, social difficulties and difficult-to-manage behavior. The social dysfunction and peer rejection seen in children with ADHD may be distinguished from the social isolation and indifference to facial and tonal communication cues seen in ASD children. Children with ADHD may misbehave or have a tantrum during a major transition in their lives because of impulsivity or poor self-control. In contrast, ASD children may throw tantrums as they fail to tolerate a change from their expected course of events.

ASSESSING YOUR CHILD

Most children tend to seek medical attention after they have entered primary school where they are expected to perform well, get along with peers and behave in a socially acceptable way.

The diagnosis for Attention Deficit Hyperactivity Disorder (ADHD) is a clinical one based on diagnostic interview methods with the child and his family. There is no definitive diagnostic test for ADHD, but the clinical interview is one of the cornerstones of the assessment process.

6.1   WHAT DO DOCTORS LOOK OUT FOR?

Doctors look out for certain signs and symptoms, the foremost being significant distress or impairment in at least two social situations. These could be family relationships, interactions with classmates at school or behaviour in other social settings. The symptoms that the child displays—of inattention, hyperactivity and impulsivity—should not only disruptive, but they should also be inconsistent with his developmental levels.

Next, doctors make sure that the symptoms are not caused by other mental disorders like depression or anxiety. The symptoms should also have been around for at least six months.

Finally, doctors look for any hearing or eye defects as these conditions may be the cause of the child's inattention.

6.2   IS THERE A SPECIAL BLOOD TEST OR BRAIN SCAN THAT CAN DIAGNOSE ADHD?

There is no special blood test or brain scan that doctors can use to diagnose ADHD. Although several regions and structures of the brains of children with ADHD are consistently smaller than the brains of children without ADHD, the difference is too small for doctors to make a diagnosis.

6.3   WHAT ARE RATING SCALES AND ARE THEY USEFUL IN DIAGNOSING ADHD?

Rating scales consist of items that reflect the symptoms of the disorder. Examples of these items are making careless mistakes in schoolwork or often failing to give close attention to details.

These items are rated by the child's parent or teacher on a four-point scale of "Not at all", "Just a little", "Pretty much" or "Very much", and given a score of say

1, 2, 3 or 4. A total score beyond a certain cut-off point, which is predetermined as valid for the scale, would indicate the likelihood and severity of the disorder.

Rating scales of ADHD cannot replace the clinical assessment but may be used, in doubtful cases, to add some rigour, standardisation and a quantifiable dimension to the areas being evaluated. If used before and after drug treatment, rating scales might help clinicians to gauge the degree of change in the symptoms, be they for the better or the worse.

6.4 WHY DO DOCTORS ASK ABOUT SCHOOL AND FAMILY LIFE?

Doctors may explore the child's functioning and behaviour in different settings and from different sources like teachers and other child-care workers. This is because it is possible that children behave very differently in different settings.

For example, a child with a learning problem or disorder is more likely to show disturbed and inattentive behaviour in the classroom than in the home. Conversely, a child who has relationship difficulties with his parents is more likely to show misbehaviour at home but may be reported by teachers to have exemplary conduct in school.

Doctors also need to evaluate the school and home situation because children with ADHD do worse in chaotic environments and are much more difficult to discipline effectively. Many children with ADHD also have concurrent learning disorders.

6.5 WHAT DO DOCTORS NEED TO FIND OUT FROM THE FAMILY OF THE ADHD CHILD?

Doctors will ask parents to describe the onset, development and extent of the child's symptoms in relation to his academic, social and emotional functioning. They will inquire about the child's birth and look out for any incidents (like head injuries, meningitis, asthma or febrile fits) or the use of medications (such as antihistamines, betaagonists and phenobarbital) that might have affected the child's attention span.

Doctors will also conduct a careful and extensive inquiry into the mental well-being of the child's parents and extended family members. They will explore the family situation and look out for evidence of parental stress and psychosocial adversity such as poverty, family conflicts and illness.

6.6   ARE REPORTS BY TEACHERS USEFUL?

Reports given by teachers are invaluable. This is because teachers spend a great deal of time with their students and are able to observe them closely. Moreover, as most teachers have extensive experience in teaching and dealing with children, they have a good understanding of childhood behaviour and development. Reports by teachers also tend to be more objective than reports given by parents.

6.7   MY CHILD IS ONLY 4 YEARS OLD. HIS TEACHERS COMPLAIN THAT HE CANNOT PAY ATTENTION. CAN THE DOCTOR DIAGNOSE MY CHILD TO HAVE ADHD?

It is possible to make a diagnosis of ADHD in very young children. But doctors usually make such a diagnosis cautiously as there are developmental disorders, such as delay in language development especially in boys or adjustment disorders, that may present a picture similar to that of a child with ADHD.

Most children with ADHD start to have serious disruptive or inattentive behaviour when they enter primary school, where the demands of academic study are very different from their carefree preschool days. These children are spotted by teachers who inform the parents to take the child to see a doctor.

6.8   I AM WARY OF PUTTING MY CHILD ON DRUGS AS I FEAR THEY MIGHT ALTER HIS MIND FUNCTIONS. WOULD MY CHILD BE SUBJECT TO TREATMENT WITH MEDICATION?

Medication is not used as a first option. In fact, medication is used as a last resort, when the child fails to respond to other non-medication methods of treatment or when the disruptions caused by the child is extremely disturbing or troublesome. In these cases, medication can help reduce unwanted behaviour and lead to improved relationships with parents, teachers and peers.

Doctors would most usually prescribe behavior management and modification therapy as well as psycho-educational interventions as a first option.

TREATING YOUR CHILD
WITH MEDICATION

PART 7

The most commonly prescribed drug for children and adolescents with Attention Deficit Hyperactivity Disorder (ADHD) is methylphenidate (trade name: Ritalin). This is a psycho-stimulant drug that is used to treat mental disorders in children. Its use continues to accelerate as ADHD gains acceptance and increasing recognition worldwide.

Other commonly used medications are anti-depression, anti-psychotic, anti-anxiety and mood-stabilising drugs.

7.1 WILL PSYCHO-STIMULANT MEDICATIONS CAUSE DAMAGE TO MY CHILD'S BRAIN AND AFFECT HIS ABILITY TO STUDY?

Psycho-stimulant medications, such as methylphenidate, are safe and effective first line agents prescribed for children with ADHD. In therapeutic dosages, they do not cause damage to the brain. They are also not known to cause addiction.

Over 170 studies regarding the use of methylphenidate have been carried out on more than 5,000 children between the ages of 5 and 12. Most of these studies were conducted in the US. In these trials, patients were randomly assigned to one of two groups — medication group and placebo group. The results were analysed to see if there were any significant differences in the outcome of the two groups. The results show that methylphenidate:

- safely reduces the core symptoms of ADHD in the short and intermediate term,
- improves functions in a number of areas, including behaviour in the classroom and other social situations.

However, these studies have not been shown to be able to increase the intelligence of children.

7.2 HOW DOES METHYLPHENIDATE ACT ON THE BRAIN?

The brain depends on the neuro-transmitter dopamine to function properly. When the level of dopamine in the brain is low, the brain cannot function properly and there is a so-called loss of inhibition. The child becomes inattentive, impulsive and hyperactive.

In children with ADHD, methylphenidate works directly on the chemistry of the brain in three sites: the prefrontal cortex, basal ganglia and cerebellum. It adjusts the levels of dopamine in these areas, thus restoring proper functions.

While methylphenidate alters the functions of the brain, it does not alter the structures of the brain and hence it does not cause brain damage.

In many cases, children treated with methylphenidate show an improved relationship with their parents and friends. Their performance in school also improves. Ultimately, their confidence is boosted and self-esteem is raised.

7.3   WHAT ARE THE SIDE EFFECTS OF METHYLPHENIDATE?

Methylphenidate causes some side effects but these are generally mild and can be managed by adjusting its dosage or the time it is taken.

Common side effects include:

- loss of appetite,
- insomnia,
- irritability,
- abdominal pains,
- headaches,
- loss of weight in some children.

Studies show that there is no significant impact on the child's potential height. Although there are some clinical reports of increased motor tics and becoming over-focused (inability to think laterally and restricted in thinking abilities), these other side effects have not been consistent across studies.

It is important to note that these side effects usually occur early in treatment and may decrease with time. When adverse reactions do occur, they are usually related to dosage levels and are always reversible when the dose is reduced. With careful therapeutic use and when given under medical supervision, the long-term use of methylphenidate has not shown to be harmful.

7.4   AS METHYLPHENIDATE IS A STIMULANT, WILL MY CHILD BECOME DEPENDENT ON IT?

Although studies have shown that children with ADHD are at a higher risk for drug abuse and cigarette smoking, this risk appears to be associated with the ADHD condition itself rather than the drug. In a study jointly funded by the National Institute of Mental Health and the National Institute on Drug Abuse in

Maryland (US), boys with ADHD who were treated with stimulant drugs were significantly less likely to abuse drugs and alcohol when they became older. Moreover, on taking methylphenidate, children do not describe any euphoria as is usually reported by adults. This is because the dosage that children receive is strictly controlled. Addiction to the drug can occur only if it is taken in high doses and over a prolonged period, and this is not possible when children are medically supervised.

Despite the concerns that ADHD may increase the risk of drug abuse in adolescents and young adults, there is a paucity of scientific data to support this fear. To sum up, well-established findings show that it is more advantageous for the child to seek medical treatment for ADHD than to avoid treatment.

7.5   IS THERE A STANDARD DOSE FOR METHYLPHENIDATE?

Methylphenidate is available only on prescription and in doses ranging from 10 mg to 60 mg a day. The dosage prescribed depends on the child's:

- body weight,
- severity of symptoms,
- individual sensitivity to the drug.

The dose may be split up and taken two or three times a day. The effects of each dose lasts from four to six hours. Doctors do not recommended that children take more than 60 mg a day.

Depending on the needs of the child, doctors commonly prescribe the drug only during the school week and not on weekends and school holidays. However, some doctors would put children with ADHD on the drug daily if they needed to focus on their work and other activities.

7.6   MY CHILD MAY FORGET TO TAKE HIS MEDICATION AT THE PRESCRIBED TIMES. IS THERE A DOSE THAT CAN BE TAKEN ONCE A DAY?

Yes, it is now possible to take a slow and sustained release of methylphenidate. There are several preparations and one such drug is Concerta. The effects of this single dose is immediate and can last up to twelve hours.

Note that this slow release preparation should only be used by older children and adolescents. This is because the smallest presentation is a 20 mg tablet. It is also not advisable to break the tablet into half as this will affect its efficacy.

7.7   HOW LONG WOULD MY CHILD HAVE TO TAKE METHYLPHENIDATE?

Your child will have to take methylphenidate until he does not need it to help him focus on his work. As children mature and set goals for themselves, and are able to consciously control their impulsivity, there will usually be less need for the drug. In general terms, the average duration a child needs to take the drug is between three and five years.

Research studies in the past 10 years have also revealed evidence that methylphenidate works just as effectively in adolescents and young adults. Depending on the severity of your child's symptoms and his progress, your child may need to continue taking the drug for a longer period.

Parents, however, may have chosen to stop giving the medication to their child for various reasons, such as when:
- they see improvements in the child,
- it is inconvenient to maintain regular visits to doctors just to get prescriptions,
- it becomes inconvenient to take the medication several times a day,
- the child experience side effects early in treatment.

It is also possible that many children may not require the medication after a year or two simply because they have improved considerably.

Whatever the reasons, it is not advisable to stop your child's medication without consulting his doctor first.

7.8   IF MY CHILD DOES NOT RESPOND WELL TO METHYLPHENIDATE, IS THERE AN ALTERNATIVE DRUG THAT CAN BE USED?

About 20 percent to 30 percent of patients do not respond to stimulants. For them, a wide range of pharmacological alternatives are available.

These include anti-depressants, like imipramine, and anti-psychotic drugs. In fact, imipramine is the second most commonly used drug. Just like methylphenidate, all these other drugs work on the dopamine neuro-transmitter to give the same effects.

Atomoxetine, marketed as Strattera, is another alternative that has become increasingly used in the treatment of ADHD, especially in those patients who could not tolerate the stimulant drugs and suffer from loss of appetite and weight. It has no abuse potential as it functions differently chemically as a noradrenergic re-uptake inhibitor. However, it takes a few weeks, about four to six weeks, for its therapeutic effects to become apparent. It has to be taken daily and its effects may be fewer than those of stimulant medications.

OTHER TREATMENTS

PART 8

Parents of children with Attention Deficit Hyperactivity Disorder (ADHD) often ask if food additives and colourings worsen symptoms in the hyperactive child and should be avoided. They also ask about the value of nutritional supplements and alternative therapies in treating their child. This section addresses these other forms of treatment.

8.1   ARE THERE ANY PARTICULAR FOODS THAT COULD WORSEN ADHD AND SHOULD BE AVOIDED?

In the early 1970s, Dr Benjamin Feingold, a paediatrician with special interest in allergies, sparked off a storm of excitement and controversy by asserting that certain foods and food additives could trigger ADHD. He prescribed dietary changes for patients with hives, asthma and other allergic reactions. He claimed that 30 percent to 50 percent of his hyperactive patients benefited from diets that were free of artificial colourings and flavourings, as well as certain chemicals such as salicylates that are found naturally in apricots, berries, tomatoes and apples. The Feingold diet gained immense popularity with thousands of troubled parents who were eager for a drug-free alternative for their hyperactive children.

However, people in the processed-food industry, child-behaviour experts and many other paediatricians were unimpressed by Feingold's claims. This was because the claims were based on personal observations and not backed by controlled studies. Despite this, further research was conducted to test Feingold's claims. More than 24 controlled trials were carried out, most of which focused on food dyes. It was found that some, but not all, children were affected by diet.

8.2   WHAT DO THE CURRENT RESEARCH SAY ABOUT DIET TREATMENT?

In 1982, the National Institutes of Health in the US convened a conference to review existing scientific research on diets and hyperactivity. Although the panel noted a major limitation of the research — most of the studies tested the effect only of dyes and not of other additives and foods that might also promote hyperactivity — it concluded that:

- food additives and certain foods do, indeed, affect a small proportion of children with behavioural problems,
- controlled studies "did indicate a limited positive association between defined (Feingold-type) diets and a decrease in hyperactivity".

At the end of the conference, the panel recommended that more research should be conducted on the link between diet and behaviour. But since then, the research done on this has been scattered.

The failure to conduct a broad range of research means that little is known about the percentage of children who respond to dietary therapy, the degree to which they respond, which children are least likely to be affected, the additives and foods that cause problems, and the best ways to use diet therapy.

8.3 MY FRIENDS TELL ME THAT THERE ARE ALTERNATIVE THERAPIES THAT CAN HELP CHILDREN WITH ADHD. IS IT ADVISABLE TO PUT MY CHILD ON ANY OF THESE?

As parents are generally worried about putting their children on medication, many are looking at alternative therapies that do not involve drugs. Some current alternative therapies that are available are acupuncture, osteopathy and sensory integration.

Acupuncture

Acupuncture, an ancient form of treatment from China, has been reported to be effective in treating children with ADHD. It entails the insertion of acupuncture needles at selected points on the scalp and body. It is believed that needling these points would regulate and harmonise the functions of the body and control the symptoms of ADHD.

Osteopathy

Osteopathy involves using the hands to apply gentle pressure on the head and other parts of the body. It is believed that by freeing up restrictions in the movement of cranial bones and manipulating the flow of cerebrospinal fluid, the natural rhythms of the central nervous system that are key to health may be restored.

Sensory integration

According to sensory integration therapists, children with ADHD may have a dysfunctional sensory system whereby certain senses over-react or under-react to stimulation from the environment. Treatment involves guiding the child through activities that challenge his ability to respond appropriately to sensory input.

The effectiveness of these therapies, and many others, have not been supported by rigorous scientific research studies. As such, parents should be cautious of these treatments and not substitute them in favour of behavioural therapy and/or medication.

8.4   WHAT ABOUT NUTRITIONAL SUPPLEMENTS THAT CLAIM TO CALM ADHD CHILDREN?

Parents should be sceptical of claims that nutritional supplements can reduce hyperactivity in children, especially if the claims are not scientifically tested, validated or proven to be of help to the majority of children with ADHD. These supplements include natural nutrients like fish oils, l-carnitine and omega-3 fatty acids. Parents should be careful about putting their children solely on such treatments for these reasons:

- there is a real risk of becoming malnourished,
- there is the risk of toxicity. Some diets or herbs may contain excessive chemicals, minerals or other substances that the body cannot break down and utilise.

So far, the success of dietary treatment is limited to a small group of children. Its widespread use and recommendation in the treatment of children with ADHD is not well supported by scientific research trials. A wholesome and balanced diet is still the mainstay and safest approach for children with ADHD.

8.5   IS IT ALRIGHT TO SEEK TREATMENT FROM TEMPLE MEDIUMS?

We do not oppose or discourage anyone from seeking spiritual or religious help. Prayers or ceremony in whatever forms are acceptable if they help to allay any anxiety or fear. While it is generally safer to seek help from an established and well-attended temple, we would always advise caution. There have been many reports of indiscriminate physical abuse of children by temple mediums in the name of exorcising the "demon" within. Parents should never compromise the safety of their children under any circumstances. We do not need to give ADHD children another dose of stress by labelling them as "offending" or "possessed by" a dirty spirit.

HOW PARENTS CAN HELP

Treating children with Attention Deficit Hyperactivity Disorder (ADHD) requires a multifaceted approach. It involves:
- behaviour management therapy (implemented by both parents and care-givers),
- psycho-educational interventions (carried out in schools),
- the use of medication.

As parents, you play a very important role in helping your child come to terms with the disorder and ensuring that proper treatment is carried out. Since much of the treatment of ADHD lies with managing the behaviour of children, you should arm yourself with the knowledge of how to manage your child's behaviour.

9.1   HOW CAN I SUPPORT MY CHILD?

A good start is for you to learn as much as possible about the disorder and to tell the child that he has ADHD. You should keep your explanations clear and factual, and caution your child not to use ADHD as an excuse for misbehaving. You should also dispel all myths and misconceptions right at the start to discourage your child from using them as grounds for misbehaving.

9.2   WHAT KIND OF HOME ENVIRONMENT SHOULD I CREATE FOR MY CHILD?

Children with ADHD need structure and routine, so it helps to reflect these in the home. Here are some tips:
- Keep distractions, such as loud music or noises from electronic games, to a minimum.
- Keep the study table tidy and free of unnecessary clutter.
- Keep commonly used items like pencils and erasers in special containers and in a fixed place. Ensure these can be retrieved easily.
- Draw up a timetable for homework and chores to avoid procrastination and arguments.

9.3   SHOULD I INFORM MY CHILD'S TEACHERS THAT HE HAS ADHD?

Yes, you should, as this will help the teachers understand your child better. Furthermore, when they know of the condition, they will cooperate more fully with the professionals who are treating your child.

Getting the support and cooperation of teachers is another step in bringing your child's problems under control. Most teachers welcome such disclosure, so you should not worry that your child will be singled out and treated badly if they know of his condition.

9.4   HOW CAN I INCREASE DESIRABLE BEHAVIOUR IN MY CHILD?

A very effective way is for you to spot the desirable behaviour, no matter how small that may be, and respond immediately with praise that is specific. You could say, "I am pleased that you spoke softly and calmly to your brother."

Make sure your praise is given as soon as the behaviour is seen so that your child is clear about what pleases you. A behaviour that is noticed and praised is more likely to be repeated as children are happy when their parents are pleased. When praising, take care not to praise the attributes of the child. For example, refrain from saying, "You are so clever!" This is unhelpful and is also likely to engender an attitude of arrogance in the child.

Other methods that positively reinforce good behaviour include the use of star charts and giving rewards such as special time with you at the park or an ice-cream treat.

It is important that you foster a close relationship with your child. Only then will he be more willing to listen to you and accept whatever punishment that you might have to mete out.

9.5   HOW SHOULD I REACT WHEN MY CHILD MISBEHAVES?

It is vital that you cope with your own emotions and not be reactive or negative towards your child. This is especially so when your child shows undesirable behaviour. It is more effective to offer positive directions as to what your child should do and can do than to focus on the negative behaviour and give him a long list of prohibited actions.

Raising your child's self-esteem should always be a priority and can be achieved by generously praising good behaviour.

9.6   HOW CAN I REDUCE UNDESIRABLE BEHAVIOUR IN MY CHILD?

In handling undesirable behaviour, you should deal with your child in the same way as you would deal with normal children. Here are some tips.

Ignore The Misbehavior

This is a powerful method, but do this only if the behaviour is not dangerous. You ignore by looking away or walking away quietly. Do not look back or show any interest in what your child will do. Keep any anxiety you might feel under control.

More often than not, parents tend to react emotionally when the child misbehaves. Unfortunately, this type of negative attention tends to produce more undesirable behaviour.

Stop Dangerous Misbehaviour Promptly

If your child is showing behaviour that might endanger himself (jumping off a flight of steps) or others (biting, kicking or hitting), then you have to stop the behaviour promptly. You can do this by:

- holding him tightly from the back with both arms so that he cannot bite, hit or kick you in retaliation,
- holding him tightly and lifting him up a little so as to reduce any forceful response that he might exert.

When holding your child, keep him in your embrace for a while and do not let go straight away. Remain calm at all times. When he stops struggling, release him slowly.

Reproach Calmly

Go to your child and look at him in the eye. Then state the misbehaviour you did not like. Be calm and keep your conversation short and specific. It is not effective to shout at a distance.

Enforce Time-Out

Remove your child to a quiet area so that he can reflect on his behaviour. Do this soon after the deed has been done. Do not argue with or allow him to bargain his way out even if his favourite cartoon was going to start soon.

9.7   CAN I PUNISH MY ADHD CHILD FOR MISBEHAVIOUR?

Why not? In instances where ignoring the misbehaviour or telling the child what not to do is not always effective, punishment will help. However, beware of using excessive punishment as its impact will quickly be lost and it might lead to physical abuse.

To avoid having to resort to punishment, set out some simple and clear rules and make sure your child understands what they are. This way, he is clear about the boundaries and what is not acceptable behaviour. Also, state the consequences for breaking the rules and what he can expect as rewards for keeping to the rules.

If you have to punish your child:

- do so consistently and immediately,
- do not give in to threats or bargain with him,
- do not allow him to make you out as an ineffective parent.

9.8   WHAT SORT OF ATTITUDE SHOULD I HAVE TOWARDS MY CHILD?

You should be hopeful and optimistic that your child is capable of changing for the better. You also need to remember that your child would still need the structure and discipline that other children of the same age can do without.

You should be realistic in your expectations and:

- look out for small steps to success,
- look for the strengths in your child,
- show genuine interest and appreciation at what your child is good at and can do,
- give tasks that are within your child's ability as success as the task will help raise his self-esteem.

When your child feels valued and loved, he is more likely to behave in a way that pleases you and the other adults he comes into contact with.

9.9   WHAT TYPE OF TRAINING CAN I RECEIVE THAT WILL HELP ME COPE?

Parenting children with ADHD is highly stressful. The clinical psychologist who attends to your child will be able to show you some practical techniques for managing behaviour such as using time-out, a point system and contingent attention (rewards based on behaviour). Once you know how to handle your child, you will be able to improve the home environment for him.

Ways to improve the attention span of your child include:
- Remove environmental noise and irritation.
- Keep the home cool.
- Establish a routine and stick to it.
- Draw up a timetable for homework and daily chores with small breaks of 10 to 15 minutes.
- Keep items that your child uses within easy reach and in a fixed place.

9.10 SPECIAL EXAM PROVISIONS

Even in the absence of a specific learning disorder, school performance and academic attainment are often impaired in a child with ADHD. In Singapore, It is possible to get approval from the Ministry of Education to have special exam provisions, such as extra time and sitting in a special room with as few candidates as possible during important examinations, such as the PSLE and O or A Levels examinations in Singapore. Use of pointers and promptings by examiners, when necessary, to remind the child to focus on the exam papers may also be granted. In some deserving cases, exemption from study of the mother tongue may be considered with the support of a medical report that includes the relevant psychological, occupational and computer test findings.

HOW TEACHERS CAN HELP

Teachers play an invaluable role in the social and academic development of children. Their role is even more crucial for children with Attention Deficit Hyperactivity Disorder (ADHD). Discuss your child's condition with his teachers and seek their cooperation.

There are a few school-based psycho-educational interventions that have been found to be effective in managing the behaviour of children with ADHD. These interventions include reducing the demands of tasks or activities, making tasks more interesting and stimulating, and providing the child with opportunities to make choices related to academic work.

10.1 WHAT ARE THE LEARNING STYLES OF CHILDREN WITH ADHD?

The learning styles of children with ADHD are often based on what they can see (visual) and what they can do (kinetic) rather than what they can hear (auditory). As such, teaching should be more interactive and play-based. Increasing visual presentations and breaking activities up into small tasks are also helpful. Conceptually, the ADHD child might be described as someone with "sharp eyes but deaf ears".

10.2 WHAT IS THE VALUE OF COMPUTER-ASSISTED INSTRUCTION?

Computer-assisted instruction holds great promise for children with ADHD. This method of learning appeals to the visual styles of learning that these children prefer. With their rich colours, interactive format (which stimulates multiple sensory modalities), specifically defined instructional objectives and immediate feedback related to task performance, computer-assisted instruction is a potentially beneficial psycho-educational tool.

10.3 WHAT STRATEGIES CAN TEACHERS USE?

In the kindergarten environment, there should be minimum distraction and a small pupil-teacher ratio. Teachers should also allow the child to do the things he is good at and praise the child for good behaviour.

At primary school, teachers should seat the ADHD child right at the front of the class and, as far as possible, away from the door and window. This minimises external distractions and also allows teachers to supervise the child closely. In short, the child should be kept "under the nose" of teachers. The child should also be surrounded by students who can be good role models, that is, students who are attentive and organised. Teachers can also implement peer tutoring. This is an effective instructional strategy where two students work together on an academic activity, with one student providing assistance, instruction or feedback to the other.

10.4 HOW CAN TEACHERS CHANNEL THE ENERGY OF THE CHILD INTO ACCEPTABLE WAYS?

Teachers can do this by getting the child to perform simple stretching exercises or sending him on small errands. The aim is to break the monotony of sitting and to help the child refocus.

Teachers can also give the child manageable responsibilities such as collecting and distributing books in the class.

A teacher's recognition of a child's capability, no matter how small the responsibility, gives the child pride and motivation and will boost his self-esteem. However, teachers have to take care not to give these children too much of the same activities as these activities may either tire them out or unconsciously be seen as a form of punishment.

10.5 WHAT CAN TEACHERS DO TO ENSURE THAT HOMEWORK IS DONE?

Children with ADHD are inattentive and easily distracted. As such, they may miss important reminders given by the teacher or may not take down notes correctly.

To minimise such occurrences, the teacher can prepare notes and give them to the child. Alternatively, the child can make his own notes and show them to his teacher for checking.

The teacher can also assign a buddy for the child. The role of the buddy may include the following tasks:

- help the child with essential school-based tasks, such as making sure the homework list has been copied correctly,
- make sure the child hands in his homework,
- clarify the teacher's instructions.

The buddy should be someone who is organised in his school work. Most importantly, the buddy should be someone who will not look down on the child.

10.6 HOW DO TEACHERS CONTRIBUTE TOWARDS THE TREATMENT OF THE CHILD?

Teachers play an increasingly important role in the child's treatment. They:

- implement behavioural therapy techniques to modify the child's behaviour, which reinforces the work that parents do with their child at home,
- implement appropriate psycho-educational interventions,
- observe and record the child's behaviour in the classroom and supply this information to the child's doctor. The information helps doctors make accurate diagnosis.

Ways To Improve Attention In The Child

- Start off with simple tasks that can be completed with success
- Break learning tasks into small steps
- Make learning interesting and interactive through the use of computers and lively visual presentations
- Teach simple organisation skills

Ways To Reduce Impulsivity And Hyperactivity In The Child

- Channel the child's energy into acceptable avenues of behaviour
- Teach the child to wait his turn before answering questions
- Establish structure and discipline in the classroom
- Allow the child to fiddle an object with his hands
- Allow room for mistakes
- Assign tasks that he can see and do (activity-based response)

WHERE CAN I GO FOR SUPPORT?

PART 11

Parents looking after children with Attention Deficit Hyperactivity Disorder (ADHD) are often anxious. They worry about how their child will behave in public, whether their child will get into trouble at school and whether their child can improve enough to complete his education. They worry if they can cope and have the energy to see the child through. Fortunately, they are not alone as there are many other families with ADHD children. In addition, parents can join a support group, such as SPARK in Singapore. The benefits of joining a support group are immeasurable—members of the group offer mutual emotional support and share practical tips on how to deal with their hyperactive children. More importantly, parents will not feel alone and distressed that they have to cope all by themselves.

11.1 SPARK IN SINGAPORE
SPARK is a parent-support group that was set up to address issues of ADHD. The acronym stands for the Society for the Promotion of ADHD Research & Knowledge. SPARK is an independent, voluntary and non-profit organisation.

11.2 WHY AND HOW WAS SPARK FORMED?
SPARK had its roots in 1998 when a parent of a child with ADHD decided to help other parents in the same situation. It began with the ADHD Parent Support Group. The group helped many parents to understand ADHD and accept the condition in their children. There soon grew a realisation that much more had to be done to raise awareness of ADHD among educators and the general public.

In response to this need, a group of parents from the Support Group joined forces and created SPARK to continue with and expand on the scope of the work done previously by the original group.

SPARK aims to:
- create public awareness of ADHD,
- help children with ADHD and their families cope,
- promote understanding and research on ADHD,
- provide support to adults who have ADHD.

11.3 HOW DOES SPARK HELP ITS MEMBERS?
SPARK organises talks on different aspects of ADHD and holds meetings for parents to get together.

SPARK also runs its own website at http://www.spark.org.sg

The website contains interesting, practical, tried-and-tested ideas that parents, caregivers and teachers can adopt for managing children with ADHD. For example, there is a template which parents can use to write to teachers to inform them that their child has ADHD. The template gives information on ADHD as well as suggestions that will help the child's teacher manage the child better in the classroom.

The website also describes strategies for coping with each of the difficulties of inattentiveness, hyperactivity and impulsiveness. In addition, the website offers a list of useful resources and the latest information on therapy and medication.

Parents are strongly encouraged to join a support group so as not to feel alone. As the saying goes, "a problem shared is a problem halved." Getting together creates a sense of camaraderie and relief that one is not unique in having a particular set of problems.

11.4 WHAT CAN PARENTS IN OTHER COUNTRIES DO?

In countries where child professionals may not be easily available, parents may use the 3As (Aware, Analyse and Advice) approach in helping children with possible ADHD.

If your child is very restless and inattentive, it helps to be aware that he may have ADHD. Next, analyse if these behaviours are pervasive and persistent for more than six months. Check if they cause distress to the caregivers and teachers, result in a disturbed relationship with the peers or affect his study and learning capability. You may reflect on whether your response to your child's misbehaviours is effective and appropriate. As a rule, parents should not be reactive by raising their voice at their child. It is seldom helpful and instead this is more likely to give the child negative attention. On the contrary, you should pay him attention and praise him when he behaves well. Thus, your child is motivated to keep up the good behaviour.

Providing a routine and structure in the daily activities of the child with participation in some games and sports would help to make him conform to the norm and learn from others in cultivating acceptable behaviours.

If these measures fail, consider seeking the advice of other parents who have similar problems or ask the school teachers for advice. The experience gained in dealing with children with ADHD by these people could be very enlightening in addition to the emotional support they provide.

WHAT KIND OF
PROFESSIONAL HELP CAN I GET?

PART 12

Children with Attention Deficit Hyperactivity Disorder (ADHD) need professional help. This help is provided by a team of mental health professionals which include doctors or psychiatrists, psychologists, social workers and specialist teachers. Mental health professionals play a big role in helping your child achieve mental well-being.

12.1 CHILD PSYCHIATRISTS

Child psychiatrists are medical doctors who receive further training in the specialised area of child mental health. They are experts on mental disorders and can manage children's problems using a biological, psychological and social approach. The child psychiatrist performs comprehensive assessments and diagnosis, and prescribes medications to treat children with ADHD.

12.2 PSYCHOLOGISTS

Psychologists are trained in psychology, which is the science of understanding human behaviour. Clinical psychologists are trained to help children with mental health problems. They provide help in the form of behaviour therapy for the child and counselling for parents.

When psychologists counsel parents, they will provide advice on how to handle their child and show them methods that can help them change their child's behaviour. Psychologists are also trained to provide IQ and psychological testing which will reveal the type and severity of the educational difficulties many of these ADHD children may have. Such testing is important as it helps to map out the appropriate remedial measures to help the child.

12.3 SOCIAL WORKERS

Social workers are concerned about the social aspects of children in relation to their family, relationships and social skills. They use family therapy and parent counselling to help the children and their families. They also conduct group sessions which provide essential social skills for children. The counselling and support that social workers provide for parents of ADHD children is extremely helpful. This is because parents also need to take care of their emotions so that they can help their ADHD child more effectively.

Social workers are also familiar with the various sources of community support services that families can tap into.

12.4 SPECIALIST TEACHERS

Specialist teachers are based in the primary schools and at the Child Guidance Clinic. Known as Learning Support Co-ordinators, these teachers provide help to ADHD children who have specific learning problems. Specialist teachers undergo training that helps them identify children with attention problems, learning problems and hyperactivity. They learn how to deal with such children and will incorporate appropriate psycho-educational interventions like computer-assisted learning in their teaching.

Parents who are worried about their child's academic performance and abilities can also seek the advice and help of these teachers.

12.5 THE CHILD GUIDANCE CLINIC (SINGAPORE)

Help is usually provided through a team approach and this is available from the Child Guidance Clinic. This is the main government clinic in Singapore that assesses and treats emotional, behavioural and developmental disorders in children and adolescents up to the age of 18 years. There are also many other privately-run clinics that provide mental health services.

12.6 WHAT CAN PARENTS IN OTHER COUNTRIES DO?

In other countries where there are few child mental health professionals, parents who strongly suspect their children may have ADHD do not have to suffer in silence. On the Internet, there is an abundance of information on ADHD and its treatment. However, one should be mindful that the accuracy of some of the methods of treatment advocated are without scientific basis. They could be potentially harmful.

Parents may talk to their trusted relatives, friends or neighbours about their problems. They may be surprised that these problems are common and they may learn and benefit from other people's considerable experience and wisdom in helping these children.

Parents may approach the school teachers for help. Support groups for parents may also be available in the community for additional help. A general practitioner should be able to provide advice and counselling for parents.

WHAT THE FUTURE HOLDS

PART 13

People with Attention Deficit Hyperactivity Disorder (ADHD) are usually extroverted, curious and energetic. On the downside, they are impatient and easily distracted.

Even then, it is a common observation that most people with ADHD can focus extremely well on something they find interesting. They also have a sense of intuition. It is not surprising that with a combination of such traits, people with ADHD can do well in vocations that involve exploration and invention. Great inventors and divergent thinkers such as Thomas Edison and Ben Franklin all exhibited traits of ADHD.

13.1 HOW HAVE PEOPLE WITH ADHD HELPED THEMSELVES?

People who have learnt to live successfully with ADHD share several common features. In particular, they are likely to:

- capitalise on their strengths and creativity,
- find ways to overcome their weaknesses,
- learn from mentors and successful individuals who have overcome their own ADHD problems,
- analyse their mistakes and constantly think of ways to better their lives,
- set short-term goals that give them the greatest chances of success.

13.2 HOW MANY CHILDREN WITH ADHD CONTINUE TO HAVE DISABLING SYMPTOMS IN ADULTHOOD?

Research findings suggest somewhere between 4 percent and 11 percent of children with ADHD continue to have disabling symptoms in adulthood.

Studies conducted on adults with ADHD has led to the introduction of a new "residual" form of the syndrome*. The belief was that adults who came to clinics complaining of concentration difficulties, restlessness, impatience, and so on had been suffering from ADHD all along since childhood. This view was further reinforced when these adults responded well to stimulant medication. However, not all investigators accept the existence of adult ADHD. There are three main arguments for this.

- First, the studies rely on making a diagnosis of ADHD in childhood based on what the adult patients currently report. This means the diagnosis is questionable.

*This new form was introduced in DSM-3 (1980).

- Second, many such studies also rely exclusively on self reports whereby there are no corroborative evidence to support or confirm what was said.
- Third, and more importantly, is that diagnosis in adulthood is a complicated issue. This is because the symptoms of ADHD can be found in many other adult mental disorders. For example, concentration difficulties can be found in major depression, restlessness can be found in generalised anxiety disorder, and impulsivity can be found in bipolar mood disorder.

13.3 WHAT HAPPENS IN THE LATE TEEN YEARS?

In their late teens, individuals with ADHD tend to perform poorer in their studies. This is particularly true for those who have learning disorders and for those who did not receive early intervention.

In the late teen years, these individuals are easily distracted and not motivated. They also have low self-esteem and because they are less socially adept, have fewer friends. In addition, a significant minority demonstrate pervasive antisocial behaviour, such as lying, truancy and even drug abuse, all of which are consistent with a conduct disorder.

13.4 WHAT CAN HAPPEN IN THE MID-TWENTIES?

With appropriate treatment, having childhood ADHD does not preclude the individual from achieving educational and vocational goals.

In fact, by the mid-20s, most children do not experience emotional or behavioural problems that can hamper them. This could be because they are more motivated and focused, and have strong support systems.

Nearly all adults who had ADHD as children are gainfully employed, with some in high level positions. Two-thirds show no evidence of any mental disorder. The characteristics of ADHD, such as high energy level, intensity, affinity for stimulating environments, if positively channelled, can be assets.

13.5 WHAT TYPES OF CAREERS ARE BEST SUITED FOR PEOPLE WITH ADHD?

Individuals with ADHD are usually creative and daring. They are also good at using their hands. They may be artistic, knowledgeable and have good computer skills.

They may also enjoy outdoor activities as well as travelling. The most suitable jobs, therefore, would be those that:
- offer a variety of activities,
- provide autonomy,
- require creative input.

Such jobs are likely to be writing, painting, designing and business. Individuals with ADHD may also adapt well in stimulating environments such as fire safety, law enforcement or the military.

13.6 WHAT VOCATIONS ARE NOT SUITABLE FOR PEOPLE WITH ADHD?

Individuals with ADHD lack patience, and have poor concentration and attention spans. They cannot focus for too long at any one time. As such, they should avoid jobs that are repetitive and monotonous, such as accounting, research and managerial work where they have to pay attention to details.

IMPORTANT RESEARCH FINDINGS

PART **14**

The Multimodal Treatment Study of Children with Attention Deficit Hyperactivity Disorder (MTA Study) is a significant study. Its findings, first published in December 1999, provide important guidance for the treatment of children with ADHD.

The MTA Study was conducted by the National Institute of Mental Health in the US. It was the first major clinical trial in history to focus on a childhood mental disorder and the largest clinical trial ever conducted by the Institute.

To evaluate the leading treatments for ADHD, the MTA Study was conducted at six different university medical centres and hospitals that are recognised for their work in treating children with ADHD.

14.1 WHY WAS THE MTA STUDY CONDUCTED?

Although ADHD is relatively common, our knowledge of the problem is incomplete. Current treatment includes a mix of approaches, such as drug therapy, counselling, supportive services in schools and communities, and various combinations of these approaches.

The medical literature that is available offers many studies but these were carried out over brief treatment periods of three months or less. A pressing question remains: what is the best kind of help we can offer ADHD children over a longer term? The MTA Study provides the answers.

14.2 HOW WAS THE MTA STUDY CONDUCTED?

Nearly 600 school children, aged from seven to nine years, were involved in the study. They were randomly assigned to one of four leading treatment modes:
- Medication alone (under the specialised care of a psychiatrist).
- Behavioural treatment alone.
- A combination of both medication and behavioural treatment.
- Routine community care (with medication prescribed by a general practitioner).

14.3 HOW WERE THE CHILDREN SELECTED FOR THE MTA STUDY?

The criteria for selecting the children were stringent. Children who had behaviour problems but not ADHD were not eligible. Investigators interviewed the children and their parents to learn more about the nature of the child's symptoms, and to rule out the presence of other conditions or factors that may have given rise to the child's difficulties.

In addition, extensive historical information was gathered and diagnostic interviews were conducted in order to establish whether or not the child exhibited the long-standing pattern of symptoms characteristic of ADHD across home, school and peer settings. Only when the child met the full criteria for ADHD and study entry (and many did not) were they and their families eligible for the study.

14.4 WHAT DOES THE MTA STUDY SHOW?

The MTA Study demonstrates for the first time the safety and relative effectiveness of two treatment methods—medication alone, and medication combined with behavioural treatment —for a period of up to fourteen months. It compares these treatments to routine community care.

The results indicate that:

- long-term combination treatments as well as treatment by medication alone are significantly superior to intensive behavioural treatments and routine community treatments in reducing ADHD symptoms,
- these differential benefits extend for as long as 14 months,
- in other areas (specifically anxiety, oppositionality, academic performance, parent-child relations and social skills), the combined treatment approach was consistently superior to routine community care, whereas the single treatments (medication only or behavioural treatment only) were not.

The combined treatment approach also allowed children to be successfully treated over the course of the study with lower doses of medication, compared to the medication-only group.

14.5 GIVEN THE EFFECTIVENESS OF MEDICATION MANAGEMENT, WHAT IS THE ROLE OF AND NEED FOR BEHAVIOURAL THERAPY?

The MTA Study has demonstrated that for periods lasting as long as 14 months, carefully-monitored medication management is more effective than intensive behavioural treatment. All children tended to improve over the course of the study. However, there were differences in the levels of improvement, with the carefully administered medication-only approach generally showing the greatest improvement. Nonetheless, the children's responses varied enormously. For children who were concerned with academic performance and familial relations, the combination of behavioural therapy and medication, rather than community care, was necessary to produce improvements. Notably, families and teachers reported higher levels of satisfaction for those treatments that included behavioural therapy.

Therefore, medication alone is not necessarily the best treatment for every child, and families often need to pursue other treatments, either alone or in combination with medication.

14.6 WHAT IS THE RIGHT TREATMENT FOR A CHILD?

There is no single treatment that will suit every child. A number of factors appears to be involved in determining which treatments are best for which children. For example, even if a particular treatment might be effective in a given instance, the child may have unacceptable side effects that might prevent that particular treatment from being used.

In developing suitable treatments for ADHD, each child's needs, personal and medical history and other relevant factors like current family situation or personal predicaments, have to be carefully considered.

14.7 THE MTA STUDY REVEALED A SURPRISE FINDING. WHAT IS IT?

One surprise finding is that children treated with effective medication management (either alone or in combination with intensive behavioural therapy) improved substantially in social skills and peer relations than children in the community comparison group after 14 months. This important finding indicates that the symptoms of ADHD may interfere with their learning of social skills and that medication may benefit many children.

14.8 WHY WERE THE MEDICATION TREATMENTS GIVEN BY SPECIALISTS MORE EFFECTIVE THAN THOSE GIVEN VIA ROUTINE COMMUNITY CARE?

Two groups of children with ADHD were studied. Although both groups were given the same stimulant medication, there were some differences in their management.

In the medication-only group:
- the psychiatrist took special care to find an optimal dose of medication for each child,
- the children were seen every month for 30 minutes each time,

- during the visits, the psychiatrist spoke with the child and his parents to determine any concerns that the family might have regarding the medication or the child's ADHD-related difficulties,
- if the child was experiencing any difficulties, the psychiatrist was encouraged to consider adjustments in the child's medication rather than take a wait-and-see approach,
- the psychiatrist sought input from the child's teacher on a monthly basis, and used this information to make any necessary adjustments in the child's treatment,
- parents were given advice concerning any problems the child may have been experiencing,
- parents were given reading materials and additional information,
- the children took their medication in three doses per day and in somewhat higher doses.

In comparison, in the routine community care group:
- the doctor generally met the children only once or twice a year,
- each visit was short,
- there was no interaction with the teachers,
- lower doses of medication were prescribed and these were taken twice a day.

The results show that there is a distinctive superior effectiveness in the medication treatment group than the routine community care group. The reasons lie in the substantial differences in the quality and intensity of the treatment they received.

USEFUL RESOURCES

Books

ADHD Parenting Guide. Janssen, a division of Johnson & Johnson Pte Ltd, 2014.

Ashley, Susan. *1000 Best Tips for ADHD: Expert Answers and Bright Advice to Help You and Your Child*. Sourcebooks Inc, 2012.

Barkley, Russell A. *Taking Charge of ADHD: The Complete, Authoritative Guide for Parents (Third Edition)*. Guilford Publications Inc, 2013.

Bertin, Mark. *The Family ADHD Solution: A Scientific Approach to Maximizing Your Child's Attention and Minimizing Parental Stress.* St. Martin's Press, 2011.

Burba, Beth and Pauline Johnson. *ADHD Parenting: Parenting ADHD Children Simple Book for Parents Raising Kids with Attention Deficit Hyperactivity Disorder.* CreateSpace Publishing, 2014.

Charter, Cheryl. *Organise Your ADD/ADHD Child: A Practical Guide for Parents.* Kingsley: Jessica Publishers, 2010.

Dendy, Chris A. Zeigler. *Teenagers with ADD and ADHD: A guide for parents and professionals.* Woodbine House, 2006.

Kutscher, Martin L. *ADHD: Living without Brakes.* Jessica Kingsley Ltd, 2008.

Quinn, Patricia O. *Attention, Girls!: A Guide to Learn All About Your Ad/Hd.* American Psychological Association, 2009.

Richey, Mary Anne. *Raising Boys with ADHD: Secrets for Parenting Healthy, Happy Sons.* Sourcebooks Inc, 2012.

Shapiro, Lawrence. *The ADHD Workbook for Kids: Helping Children Gain Self-Confidence, Social Skills, and Self-Control.* New Harbinger Publications, 2010.

Websites

ADD RESOURCES Information, Services and Support For ADHD
www.ADDresources.org

ADHD Support
www.ADHDSupportcompany.com

American Academy of Child and Adolescent Psychiatry
http://www.aacap.org/aacap/Families_and_Youth/Resource_Centers/ADHD_
Resource_Center/Home.aspx

Attention Deficit Disorder Association
www.add.org

CADDRA Canadian ADD ADHD Research Association
www.caddra.ca

CHADD Children and Adults with ADHD
www.chadd.org

Child Guidance Clinic
www.imh.com.sg

National Institute of Mental Health
www.nimh.nih.gov

Society for the Promotion of ADHD Research and Knowledge
www.spark.org.sg

The Complete ADD/ADHD Bookstore
www.add411.com

ABOUT THE AUTHOR

Dr Cai Yiming graduated from the University of Singapore in 1975. He joined Woodbridge Hospital (now known as Institute of Mental Health) as a medical officer and started his career in psychiatry in 1977. He received postgraduate training in psychiatry at the Institute of Psychiatry in London under a Commonwealth Scholarship (United Kingdom) from 1979 to 1981. He has been a Fellow of the Academy of Medicine (Singapore) since 1987.

From 1991 to 1992, Dr Cai was based in the Hospital for Sick Children, Toronto (Canada) as Clinical Fellow under the Health Manpower Development Plan Fellowship Scheme (Ministry of Health, Singapore). He was Head of the Department of Child and Adolescent Psychiatry at the Institute of Mental Health from 1993 to 2006.

In 1999, Dr Cai was appointed as a WHO Consultant on Life Skills Education for school children.

He is an examiner for the post-graduate M. Med (Psychiatry) Examination, National University of Singapore.

He was a recipient of the 2007 National day award in Public Administration Medal (Bronze). In 2010, he was a winner of the Healthcare Humanity Award by the National Healthcare Group and received the Long Service Award on the National Day. He was awarded the National Healthcare Group Outstanding Citizenship Award in 2011 and conferred the title of Emeritus Consultant by the Institute of Mental Health in 2014.

Dr Cai has written several books. He co-authored:
- *Help Your Child to Cope: Understanding Childhood Stress* (1998), and
- *Raise Your Child Right: A Parenting Guide for 0-6 Years* (2002), both published by Times Editions.
- *Health Wise*, a series of Health Education Textbooks for Primary School Children, published by Federal Publications, 2001.

He has also written several books:

- In 2002, he wrote *When Two Elephants Fight* (2002) published by the Institute of Mental Health, Singapore.
- In 2003, he wrote *Living with ADHD* (2003). This is a book on Attention Deficit Hyperactivity Disorder published by Times Editions International.
- In 2005, he wrote *When Parents Fight, The Children Cry*, published by Hope Story publishers.
- In 2008, he co-edited and contributed a number of chapters in the book, *A Primer of Child and Adolescent Psychiatry,* which was published by World Scientific Publishing.

Dr Cai is currently an Emeritus Consultant Psychiatrist, Department of Child and Adolescent Psychiatry and Advisor, Department of General and Forensic Psychiatry at the Institute of Mental Health, Singapore.